3.95
11702

Books by Jean Valentine
DREAM BARKER
PILGRIMS
ORDINARY THINGS

Ordinary Things

JEAN VALENTINE

ORDINARY THINGS

FARRAR · STRAUS · GIROUX
NEW YORK

Some of these poems first appeared in American Poetry Review,
Arion's Dolphin, Field, Harper's Magazine, The Iowa Review,
Kumanitu, The Ohio Review, Swarthmore Alumni Bulletin, and
Unmuzzled Ox. Three poems—"After Elegies," "After Elegies
(2)," and "Anaesthesia"—first appeared in Antaeus.

Library of Congress Cataloging in Publication Data

Valentine, Jean.
   Ordinary things.

   Poems.
   I. Title.
PS3572.A3907   811'.5'4   74-11452

With deep thanks to The Kendall Foundation,
The National Endowment for the Arts,
and the Creative Artists Public Service Program;
to The Corporation of Yaddo,
and The Cummington Community of the Arts.

for Sarah and Beka

Contents

Contents

Chalk lines still mark the floor
just where you stood. Our shoulders touched.
I was afraid. You were just saying
ordinary things.

—Huub Oosterhuis, *Twenty Days' Journey*

1

After Elegies

Almost two years now I've been sleeping,
a hand on a table that was in a kitchen.

Five or six times you have come by
the window; as if I'd been on a bus

sleeping through the Northwest, waking up,
seeing old villages pass in your face,

sleeping.
          A doctor and his wife, a doctor too, are in the kitchen
area, wide awake. We notice things
differently: a child's handprint in a clay plate, a geranium,
    aluminum
balconies rail to rail, the car horns of a wedding,

blurs of children in white. *LIFE* shots
of other children.   Fire to paper; black

faces, judge faces, Asian faces; flat
earth   your face   fern   coal

"Autumn Day"

Who has no house now will not build him one . . .
Will waken, read, and write long letters . . .
—RILKE, *Autumn Day*

The house in the air is rising, not
settling between any trees.
Its lines may have come here by machine,
wirephoto, they soften to dots in the rain.

What draws you on so hard?
                    You would like to think
about resting
a minute on the mobbed walk or
the electrocardiograph table
                    to ask about the house there—dark,
                    stone, floating out over the edge of the buildings,
                    someone, something, it may be, inside—
but you can't stop here: the dangerous air,
the crowds, the lights, the hardening Indian Summer . . .

                    strange quiet,
with time for work, your evenings, you will write long letters
this winter, you have your friends,
and the names of friends of friends.

He said,

"When I found where we had crashed, in the snow, the two of us, alone, I made a plan. It takes all my energy to like it.
The trees keep thinning, and the small animals.
She swims over me every night like warmth, like my whole life going past my eyes. She is the sleep they talk about, and some days all I can want is sleep."

Forces

FOR E. AND V.U.

This man, blind and honored,
listens to his student reader;
this man did what he thought
and sickens in jail; another
comes to the end of his work;
another threw himself out.

Us too, our destinies get on,
into middle age.

Today we visited a field of graves—
slaves' or Indians' graves, you said—
sunk, unmarked, green edges of hammered granite
sharp as a shoulder blade.
                              God break me out
of this stiff life I've made.

Shannock
February 1972

Kin

FOR W.A.

A woman's face at the window,
white, composed, tells me I
do not love her; I did not love him;
I do not love my children, so they wither,
so she will take them, take them away.

I cannot love him: he is dead. And she—
she will not hurt us now.

But the somber child;
and the wind, and the white window.

Anaesthesia

Right after her birth they crowded in,
into the white room, huge tall masks
of women's faces

brick-red lips, chalked-in triangular eyes
gazed at us: nothing; said:
nothing; not-women they were suicides, trees, soft,
pale, freckled branches bending over her—
I knew them as my own, their cries
took on the family whiskey voice, refusal,
need, —their human need peeled down, tore,
scratched for her life—
I hacked and hacked them apart—

then who knows
when you murder things like that
who comes in and takes over

After Elegies (2)

The doctors tell me, "Swim.
You are beginning, moving on; yes,
trailing his side, still
amazed at your own body apart; yes, looking back,
you don't have to smile that way, afraid
we are not here; you are beginning,
leaving nothing; your friend is here
with you, and you know him,
and all your old desire;
but in a queer tranquillity.
Yourselves. No reason any more
why not."

2

3 a.m. in New York

FOR A.V.C.

I have been standing at the edge
of this green field all night.
My hand is sticky with sugar.

The village winks; it thinks it is
the muscle of the world. The heart.
The mouth.

The horse is standing across the field, near the fence.
He doesn't come any closer,
even in the dark, or run away.

Blood memory:
fixed on vacancy:
coming back and back for a sign

the flat of his coat
the shut out of his eye.

Space

Keeping to my room
the cut in my thumb
took on more interest than the thumb

the dark a clean success
after the changing mask
of his face,

and my body—
its hypnotic
ticking over and over,

wanting, not wanting,
in all that hard-edged, squared-off, positive
concrete, aluminum.

I let it go,
all seven years and seven years.

I'm weightless, free   unwritten space

How do they get from minute to minute here?

Far off, low,
a little stir begins, a word, a missed

beat, a listening: this-
world, this-world.

Letter from a Country Room

Off without you
I hang around in the middle distance, walking, talking,
working   made-up mindwork
to send to the city Michael
where you are, where you write
        "She's coming back from the coast next week,
        I don't know what then"
A moth beats at the screen,
the thin, yellow dotted curtain lifts, tacked to the soft
scribbled-over wood   *signed QB + FB*   8/15-(69)
                    Nothing   *Fuck War*
                        To   *No Peace, Jaybo?*
                Worry About
The sky streams hollowness, no city cover of light.
I follow, where they go,
someone's house,
I go, dim, incognito: tacked
to the way things are. Everything streams:
dumbstruck, stopped stock-still: you too: Jaybo!
Our quiet
trustful sides
pro
tec
ted
anyhow down the whole 200 miles.

A Child's Death

I remember the dark spaces,
black sand islands rising on the x-rays:
what I couldn't touch.

Not like this world,
our old solid,
where we multiply;

not this blurred body
merely her history.

Revolution

Here is a man.
Behind him
dark, in front of him
dark. The fuse the world lit
races up his spine. Blows up
his son who holds by him,
his love of women,
his learning   his wanting
late now to be touched   to touch.
An ordinary man. Thou
red black white slight scattered

thing o women's animal-song o slant
blown up drift arch dead white
song white powder   women rocking rocking
nowhere to lay your head
fox bird woman and man
o come   and out of nothing   whiteness
they come, tearing their shirts off,
alone, together, touching,
not touching, friends, who are the living
who were the dead?

Three Voices One Night in the Community Kitchen

A MAN:

"Jeb was hitting her in the face. I sat there, not doing anything.
Her face was open, as if he wasn't hurting her. He didn't look angry.
He sat back and they were smiling at each other. He knew her
better than I did. I wanted to kill Jeb, I didn't even get up. I haven't
even said what really happened."

A WOMAN:

"I was sitting in the back seat. Another woman we both knew, but
an old friend of his, was sitting in the front seat beside him. He was
shouting at her. She wanted me to help her, to get out, but then it
changed. She was alone in the car with him. He was driving.
She tried to touch his shoulder, he shrugged her off, he was looking
straight ahead, singing, talking to the drivers of the other cars."

A MAN:

"The books are all wrong. Besides you've never read them.
"You are another person.
"I've told you all about it, maybe you don't remember.
"I had a very long, very sad dream I just wanted to see a human
     face."

The Knife

In my sleep:
Fell at his feet   wanted to eat him right up
would have   but
even better
he talked to me.

Did I ask you to?
Were those words my blood-sucking too?

Now I will have a body again
move differently, easier   back to the plan
a little house   a woman and a man

crossed against yours my soul will show
glow through my breastbone:
Back down into the kitchen
yours

Here   I will save you
others have failed, even died, but I
will save you   you save me   devour me away
up

Woke up:
I can cry but I can't wake up
today again   don't answer the door
then did   couldn't look at you   talk

couldn't place the bed in the room, or where the room was
when I closed my eyes

This is the same old knife   my knife
I know it as well as I know my own mouth
It will be lying there on the desk if

I open my eyes I will know the room very well
there will be the little thrown-out globe of blood we left
and every molecule of every object here will swell
with life. And someone will be at the door.

Seeing L'Atalante

(DIRECTED BY JEAN VIGO, 1934)

A woman sits at her worktable, reading stories,
thinking of all the true stories she'd never tell
out of love, and shame, root fear: broken glass, torn walls.
Reading stories about rivers (she is the river),
rafts crossing over, father, husband, lover,
her own sons. The river sings; he has always thought that. Stories.
The stories cross over.

On the raft he makes a shelter
for her, fills a glass (sees her trembling, clear),
tries to sleep.
Hours, hours, is he sleeping or swimming. Save her, save
them, leave them alone, his voice beats, his lungs, his heart,
his arms beat, beat, so slowly,   the wavering dark and the dark is
smiling, wanting their smile, their faces for its own.

3

TWENTY DAYS' JOURNEY
BY HUUB OOSTERHUIS
TRANSLATED FROM THE DUTCH
WITH JUDITH HERZBERG

*Huub Oosterhuis is well known in Holland for his poetry
and prose works.* Twenty Days' Journey *is taken from*
Herschreven gedichten, *poems 1955–1970.*

*The distinguished Dutch poet Judith Herzberg made
the literal English translation which I used to get at
this version of the poem.*

To them both, my deep admiration and thanks.

Twenty Days' Journey

1

I thought   it's only a thin threshold
a step scattered with straw.

It is a vertical stairway
a desert   steep with pyramids.

I edge down slopes. Dead bodies
shrug down past me. All their books.
Sentenced world, poisoned dream,
you are the most alone, the meanest.

The key I hold on to melts in my hand
I dig a pit
walk on   turn back
not a track anywhere
I bend to the wind
stalk this earth
hate my feet.

2

Wearing a veined marble vest
I sit at the game table, play,
play for life or death

for the blown-away footstep
in the snow
the voice that called me.

3

Who stumbles across the broken
field grass (foreground, left) and onto
the wide rusted wheel   falls   and then spins
and then stops   tries to think   runs on
across an island   am I.

The one who lies across the huge gold dome
(top center)   who lies   lips stretched to bursting
is you. Someone is still between us   almost
flesh   almost visible
tipped at the bottom of a blue-
brown river   like an old bottle.

4

Flood me then
stone that rushes red through the dam
fear tomorrow this moment
dry wood of imagining
dim awareness of *then*   now torn open
skinned alive.
My mind is lead, every cell
hard, heavy, metallic.

I climb up onto a road   trip
over the edge, fall
into your glass depth
you   beaker filled with fire

my body turns to mist but still stays alive,
an eye that will not close

5

20 days' journey: I pack vapor   fold air
make etchings of water on water
—see you standing there
but without a face   diamond death.

6

You are splintered into me
bits of soft denture
biting into my lips
useless pain   I am nothing   a brain pan
a cup holding your voice.
The chipped scales of your skin
crust my eyes closed
your palate slowly grows
into my mouth
your face grows out of my pores
like a feverish rash.
As if I never was
you cut your way out through every part of me
I become flesh of your flesh
bone of your bone.

7

Chalk lines still mark the floor
just where you stood. Our shoulders touched.
I was afraid. You were just saying
ordinary things.

Much became little   the mail
was left lying for days.
Nowhere now—
my sense of you everywhere

8

When they fired from the sea
onto a town
then   where the dead
stood on end like ropes
then   with the firing on Khe Sanh
it was then.

When a thin sac drifted down
out of the sky   hurled pillars
hands spattered   you called me

You had been living there a long time
you were taken
eyelids lips fingers and all
thrown against me
you   a bridge   a path through death.

I stood out in the sea, up to my waist in water
and took pictures of the fragments
the playing field   like a man's back.
The skipping survivors.

9

In small patches
it has clotted
become glass

something like a house
but empty

a shape
under a bright silk scarf.

I rub sand
into my eyes
so I won't see anything.

I hear you walk
as if you were carrying something:

your feet
grown back.

10

We walked
along the sea
the coastline broke like a thread.

I rang for days at the door
a long talk going on and on
through me like a wire

I crawled to the roof
where you were
when I got there you were gone.

4

This Hate

It is like a fitting room only
with eight or nine
mirrors instead of three—

only, no door.
But you see: no ceiling. They never do.
I love them, my mother, my daughter. Both. I do, and I can write it
out and seal it

but it hurts, the mirrors closing in.
Now: the stamp.
I have to do this very carefully,
looking up; I feel, you see, the fontanel's   gentle
beat   at closing.

Carefully now—the shine is blinding—
I have to jump and drop it out, over.

Now I need a skin.
Or maybe this fogging up
transparency is it. Is it?
It feels like yours, more or less;
only for the face.

This Minute

The videotape runs
silent, but life-size.
A bed. A woman
and a man. A woman

and a man.
A woman and a woman.
An old man and a child.
A boy and a middle-aged woman.
Two women and a man
upside-down one
woman and two men

—The long black torn shades in the classroom
flicker like pigeons. The A/V man or his boy
shuts the windows.
—Coney Island   blurred
density   a still.

A bed again, a man
alone holding himself
there. Now a woman
sitting on the bed alone

writing on a filmstrip,
I'll ask when it's over
I think but
it starts over

with this time
—did they last time?—real

faces and breasts and
hands and crotches and

I stay to see it again
to see if it's me writing
it, that woman at the end,
that might make it easier or

not. Or I might be
one of the others.
Or not. —A siren goes by
down on the street, stiffening our spines. —No I'm not her

or anyone in it at all but here
it starts over and this time
—were they last time?—
all my friends.

You're in it this time,
and me, too,
but each off   alone   clear
in the shot that was a still,

Coney Island, but animated
now, walking
smoking
playing the transistor radio.

Watching, you
touch my hand

with the hand not holding the radio and say
you never loved me so much

as this minute. The A/V man
switches on the light, says "Quiet!" and I see
all our friends are here
watching. And here it starts over.

Couvre-Feu: *after Paul Eluard*

(in peacetime)

What could you expect
we were in a strange city, we saw no one,
we had almost no money, it was cold,
we went by different names, we hoped to see no one,
we went out mostly at night, it was cold,
what could you expect
on the streets they were all going home, carrying flowers,
every paper said you are doing these things
for the last time, every silence said
this has nowhere to go,

The green walls held.
We know what we knew
what could you expect
the narrow city
shone in all night on our room
what could you expect
we were one flesh one bone.

Fidelities

Up in this quiet room here, reading your letter,
it's as if I'm in your house. I'm reading.
You're working late, downstairs. The children are all asleep.
It's raining. Later we'll have some warm bourbon and water,
and sleep.
              Outside, the streets are white, the rain
shines like glass. Police
cruise by. You hold me in your arms.
Huge planes move off overhead.

It's as if
if I answer your letter I'll have to show them
my passport: New York. October.
Other friends, another life. It's as if I could choose.

2

strange, sad, these letters

not knowing what you're thinking, reading this

Friendships, fidelities.
Things as they are.
              Out in the Sheep Meadow
I stare at the high school lovers lying, hardly moving, their skin
shining under the gray trees; I stare
at the old people, talking together, their faces
up to the sun. As if they were talking in bed.

My hand lying open in your hand . . .

The Sunday papers   the dreamy bicycle-riders

                                                  As things are
I hate, I want to embrace the man, the woman who is near you,
who hears your step.

3

not even knowing where you are

Your quick, hunched-forward walk
in this man's walk, your eyes
in that old woman's gray, restless eyes.

4

We have our lives.

The river shone white-yellow under the yellow sky; every insect
          shone,
rising and dropping. We walked back up the field to the house.

Your room there. This white room. Books, papers, letters.
Stamps, the telephone. Our lives.
We're always choosing our lives.

5

All night I thought I heard the phone, or a child
crying. Your face

turned into a snapshot of your face, one
from five years ago.

Your wife and I were sitting up late
in the kitchen, drinking coffee, talking like sisters.
A child cried; one of us went to her, held her.

Here, sitting up late, with a friend,
listening, talking, touching her hand, his hand,
I touch your hand. No one
says anything much. No one leaves anyone.

Susan's Photograph: "Jean—Summer 1972"

FOR S.T.

I am the razor that has been put away, also
the wrist in the photograph,
and—lately—also the photographer,
the friend, the taxi, the hospital room,
the three other women, their visitors, the flowers,
and the nurse.

At the end of that summer
I started going to paramedical school
at night. Days I still talk to my students
about all the dead
overexcitable poets; all their friends;
and the living; and show the old newsreels
where they keep leaving each other, old
people, children, soldiers; and the parades:
the general, the waving people, the black horses, the black
limousines, the mules, the tall gray puppets.

But this photograph here:
a woman in a country room, in western Massachusetts,
in peace, so sad and grained:
                              now I see you look up, outside the frame—
this room here, friends, a table, a book or two,
paper, see you have all you need,
—*even in prison you would have your childhood*—
see you go on and do what you ought to do,

it is enough, now,
anywhere, with
everyone you love there to talk to.

Outside the Frame

It is enough, now, anywhere,
with everyone you love there to talk to.

And to listen.
Slowly we can tell each other some things about our lives:
runs, rests, brief resolutions; falls, and lulls;
hard joyful runs, in certainty; dull, sweet
durances, human silences;
                        look back in at the children,
the regular, neutral flicker of their blood; pale, solemn,
long-legged animal-gods in their sleep,
growing into their lives, in their sleep.

Forces (2) : *Song*

Weeds breaking up through stone:
our hold on our own hollows, the quick,
curved line of a smile: bare, our own
ribs shelter us: a boy's cold, white
fingers around a match:
heart belling: hollow, quick,
through the live horn, the bone, to this
day, calm.

Notes

1. "*Autumn Day*": "The house in the air . . ."

   Jung's autobiography, *Memories, Dreams, Reflections*
   (Vintage, recorded and edited by Aniela Jaffé); Chapter X,
   Visions. These ten pages record Jung's visions during
   three weeks after his heart attack in 1944. Particularly: "A short
   distance away I saw in space a tremendous dark block of stone,
   like a meteorite. It was about the size of my house, or
   even bigger. It was floating in space, and I myself was
   floating in space . . . I had the certainty that I was about
   to enter an illuminated room and would meet there all
   those people to whom I belong in reality." (pp. 290, 291)

2. *Revolution*. After Pontecorvo's film *Battle of Algiers*.

3. *Susan's Photograph*: "*—even in prison you would have your
   childhood—*"

   Rilke's *Letters to a Young Poet* (W. W. Norton): "And even if
   you were in some prison the walls of which let none of the
   sounds of the world come to your senses—would you not
   then still have your childhood . . . ?" (p. 18)